WIND OVER ASHES

By the same author:

*Scar Tissue*, Some of Us Press, 1973

*Scar Tissue* (second edition), Hollow Springs Press, 1982

# WIND OVER ASHES

SELECTED POEMS BY

# LEONARD RANDOLPH

WITH DRAWINGS BY
KEN McCULLOUGH

CAROLINA WREN PRESS / CHAPEL HILL, NC / 1982

Some of the poems in this volume have appeared in *Dacotah Territory,*
*Copperhead, Hollow Spring Review of Poetry, Hyperion,* and *Epos.*


Drawings on cover and on section title pages are by KEN McCULLOUGH.
The drawing on page 57 appeared in *Studia Mystica.*


Copyright 1982 Carolina Wren Press


Library of Congress Cataloging in Publication Data

Randolph, Leonard, 1926-
    Wind over ashes.

    I. Title.
PS3568.A548W5          811'.54          82-1323
ISBN 0-932112-15-3     (pbk.)           AACR2

WIND OVER ASHES

WIND OVER ASHES

# PART ONE

THE VISITATION

Toward midnight the poems
come at him like drunken moths,
dashing against his skull,
crashing into his eyes like sodden light,
fluttering, death-like, into his ears.
Some of them are small
poems, with grey, translucent wings;
some are parts of large poems,
brown, ochre, impenetrably strong.

At last he cannot find the will
to sleep, arises, lights a cigaret.
The bright flare of the match
in the ticking room
destroys them.  They lie at his feet;
he steps among them like a fancy dancer,
studies them for hours in the dull
glow of cigarets.

Smoke flies from his lungs.
His nostrils flare like a dog's nose
circling to find a place to lie down.
A jet of smoke hangs frozen in midair,
becomes a poem.  There are poems everywhere
around him, on the bureau, on the windowsill,
in the dust beneath the carpet on the floor,
in the lint clustered in the bedsprings.

As morning comes, he knows, at last,
what he must do.  He will pick them up,
holding them gently, like tiny, furry animals
from the field, cupping his hands
about them, placing them carefully

upon a soft grey cloth,
impale them with gold pins,
put them under glass,
preserve them, lock them in cases
with the proper humidity controls.

He will leave them in this room,
where they belong.

He will visit them on Sundays,
in the afternoon.

SCARS

Pain is the other side
of happiness.
Often, in the dark night of the soul,
we do not know which holds us
keeps us and sustains us.
Even joy pains us when we walk from it
and deny it.

We live, at best,
day after day,
carrying the scars of love
and pain
our own stigmata
into crowded bars
and movie houses
playing reruns of the old
familiar pain
and joy
the tenderness of scar tissue
peeled slowly from the slicing wound
love left.

Scars
we are all covered with them
or
they cover us
our bodies
our minds
our hands and fingers
scarred by the fists of those we loved
scarred by caring
and being uncared for or about.

Scars of willfulness
and of despair
deep slashing scars of love
and love's burning.
We are walking scar tissue
built upon bone, love by love,
hate by hate, hurt by hurt,
until there is nothing left but scars.

There is such contentment in knowing
that, no matter what knife, what instrument
may fall into the hands of others
it cannot cause us more than pain or less
than love or leave us anything but
scars.

# THE DREAM FATHER

Light, as in a dream,
Shining about my father,
Your father,
Whose voice, like light,
Breaks about the room
Of my body, breaking
Upon the walls in shards,
Falling upon the floor,
Glistening like light,
Upon the doorknob,
Shining, like light in a dream,
Splintering upon the arms
And hands of my mother,
Drawing blood, paper slices
Cutting the fingers, clotting
On the cloth of her poor arms,
Caking on my forehead,
Gleaming, like light upon ice,
Shimmering, with that inner fire
Of light, dream-like, waiting,
Wavering in beams of light,
Waking to my own voice,
Washing out, like light in a dream,
Lost, half-lost, half-life of light
In early mourning.

As, in a dream,
Light breaks,
Sleep breaks
And we are father,
Brother, son,
Are broken light
As light, cutting, in a dream.

## SILENCES

A wool scarf.
A heavy quilt
made by a dozen hands,
withered now as their hands were,
frayed as their greying hair.
A closed room
wrapped in slow, insistent rain.
Mist and fog
shroud the morning sun.
Slowly the top of the mountain
rises out of silence,
its snow ridges
float in the air
like ghostly promises.

MORNING

Wind from the West
scatters the tall clouds
over the Olympics.

There are rumors of rain
in Seattle.  A five-car
wreck between Sequim and Chimacum
hits the early-morning news
like scattershot—one killed,
three injured, four killed, seven
injured, Sequim police report
no serious injuries.  Slowly, as
the morning moves on its course toward noon
the dead are reincarnated, the injured healed.

A light boat turns over in Discovery Bay.
The news of winter is good.
Not much snow or rain, temperatures
ranging higher than normal for November
December and January.

A fire breaks out like small arms fire
on the West slope of the Cascades.

Tomorrow is Sunday.
The small church on the hill
will entertain the Faithful
with stories of damnation
and impending purgatory.

The straits are calm.
The winds are rising.

NIGHT

There is a song that comes,
often near midnight.  It is not
like music, so much as moaning,
a low, wordless, dream-like
sound that fills the room,
cutting through the grey residue
of cigarets and burnt food.

The loose pile of dirty clothes
in the corner becomes a sculpture.
A stack of dishes
catches the light from the ascendant moon,
becomes an omen of the morning,
an obelisk to fate and danger.

Such common things—
the stench of a rotting potato
in the bin beneath the sink—
an over-ripe tomato leeches
its crystal blood onto the windowsill—
dried dill in a brown paper bag
hangs upside down from a wire
strung from the ceiling—
braided garlic dusts another wall.

Out of this meager, convex, concave environment
we do not anticipate
philosophy or love or hate.
No more than detail,
the commonplace counting clock,
the dull edge of precise existence, bound
by hanging moons, dried herbs
and dying vegetation.

PERSONA

We learn who we are
And what we mean
From what we hear
From where we've been

We know ourselves
As others know
When no one answers
When no one calls

When letters cease
And phones are still
When no steps come
On the stairs below

When cars go by
And do not stop
When breathing fills
The lone room full

And Night, the blanket
Of our childhood dream
Makes daylight die
And lies of what may seem

CLOSING OUT

The time sucks at our ears
and eyes like mesa wind,
We mark out our days
as homesteaders walked
the metes and bounds
of their new land.
When the news comes,
we do not listen.
There is too much of it.
Despite interpretation
we do not understand.
Nothing we perceive
remains within us.
We are fragments
caught in wind;
rocks flying in flooding rivers.

Day follows day.
There is no night.
The Russians are eating
our daily bread.
The President is on television.
We cannot listen.
We have heard too much of it.
We sit in silence
in a tunnel of wind
and rocks and flying water.
We mark the thimble of our days
as men on death row
waiting for the judge's hammer.

The Governor is dead.
                    There can be no appeal.

# RESPONSES

1.
Now listen.  I must tell you this.
The gathering you have come upon
is not a farewell, or a beckoning.
The opening beyond us, in the trees,
is not a gesture toward another time
or world.
          These trees remain,
are always trees, even when they are paper
and are poems
          and are filed away
in blind libraries and left unseen, unread,
as trees, unread,
interpreted
by dreams.


2.
Now the music begins.
The singers' mouths are open.
They do not sing.
The dancers gather at a grotto
in the side of the hill.
They do not dance.
The audience stares absently
at the conductor.
And he, in turn, gestures
to the violinists, the violists,
the glittering brass of the ensemble.
They do not play.


3.
You must know this: the rains will come.
The trees will fall.  The giant mills

will belch their supple sulphur
like the Styx and steam
will rise in the morning, chilling to yellow dew.
Remember, memory is like this: no sound, no music,
no dance.
       Call this much of life to memory, this silence.
Let it stay, like porcelain, behind smoked glass.

# SEARCH

Run to the end of the road, little child,
Down where the wind has grown wintry and wild,
Down where the ditches are filling with water,
Search for the willow,
Search for the father.

Search for the father,
The bend of the willow,
Down where the shadow of laurel and laughter
Twists in a turning quarrel, beguiled
By the footsteps of fathers
In search of the child.

THE SPUR

Something hot,
a sudden flash
of fire in his fingers.
Pressing the lock
of his memory
he saw the spur
and the spore erupting
the shrapnel
of memory
bites at his thigh.

He hears the scream
of mortar shells

The spur scrapes at the side
of his mind.

PERFORMANCE

Wait until you hear me
whistle.  I can dance.
I do great improvisations.
I have written words
for governors and senators
and would-be kings.
I juggle with the grace
of fools and jesters.
I know Shakespeare
like I know my thumb.
Name the great parts, all
of them, and I have done
them, not only frequently,
but well.  I have worked
with great actors and with
small directors, all in good
grace and with kindred accomplishment.
There is no book I could not have
written, no part I could not play,
no drama I could not review with
perfect judgment and grave clarity.
Wait until you hear me
whistle.

## LANDSCAPE *w/figure*

This man on the edge of the sun
whose eyes bleed sunlight
calls my name.  He is the one
man who knows my name, knows me.
I do not answer; my throat fills
with the sun; it dries and shatters
in a storm of dust; it rides the wind
into the mountains and the shadows;
it falls into the canyon and the river;
it meets the sun.  My word is lost
in sunlight, dying.  The vein in
my forehead throbs like drumbeats;
the blood climbs in my ears
and drowns in the sound of cougars
injured, crying.  I am filled
with blood, adrift in bleeding.
I touch the sun; the fire fills me.
The man on the edge of the sun
whose eyes bleed sunlight
calls my name.

In the long slow climb of the sun
in midwinter
the feather of the lark
the eagle's claw
the shadow of the hawk
settle upon me
and I am driven apart from winter
splintered away from earth and rock
left featherless
flightless
skin torn by the driving dust
of the dry summer

you
the memory
of you
falling
like a shot bird
through the bluedark summer sky
into sand
whose tongue like thistle woke within me
echoes of the rain

We care for lovers
as we care for children
wanting
in the dark hole
of our loneliness
for them to be well
to be safe
and, finding them
to be safe and well
we let our eyes bleed
on the carpet
where our fears
like ashes
turn gray
and rise as dust
and fleshlike
fall away.

PASSING

A poem is like a bird,
she says.  It spins and dips
and soars like a swallow.

Ah, no, he says.  A poem
is like an eagle.  It circles
and screams to the ground
and rips life from the underbrush.

No, the poem says.  No.
Spinning and dipping and soaring,
circling the life of language
dripping blood from its claws.

GONE

The old man
squats on a rock
at the end of
the peninsula.
He is looking
at the sea.
Tears fill
the riverbeds
of his cheeks.
I stop and
speak to him.
He does not
look at me.
I squat beside him.
He says:
My son.
Gone.
Gone? Where?
I ask.
Gone, he says.
Yes, I say.
Gone.  A grey dog
leaves him
comes to me
and lies down
with his chin
on my boot.

CENTER



The worm of darkness
coils about me.

Somewhere in the next room
I hear you speak.  One word, alone,
like a comma, suspended in space.
When I ask you
for that word
you say:

That was the answer.

Remembering the question
I know the answer
needs more than one

word.

EARNEST PRAYERS

*Petitions*

You were meditating
in the next room.

I was cooking dinner
in the kitchen.

The cream sauce began to bubble.
I turned the burner down.

The pilot light went out.
Gas filled my mouth like prayer.

WAITING

in dead winter
when I waited
for the crushed sound
of your footsteps
in the icy snow

on the sidewalk
where you waited
silent in the ice
and snow for a door
to open when a win-
dow closed upon

your footsteps
as I wait-
ed in the win-
ter in the death
of snow and ice.
and fire came
in the dead win-
ter in your foot-
steps in the ashes
of the quickly
frozen snow.

## ST. JOHN OF THE CROSS TO TERESA OF AVILA

I do not want to be thought of
as the savior of the fish

or the mender of salvation

take this piece of my flesh
and eat of it
drink this blood

and favor me with hyssop
dipped in crushed berries:
the gall in the wine of your caresses
is enough

for me

and for the fish

whose bones
I leave behind

Nothing of what you did remains
the last of the roses died this spring
the wire around the strawberries is rusted through
the moles have taken the rest of the garden
brown spots on the grass dominate the lawn
the small crack in the concrete walk
grows longer by the day
and ragweed stands like heron,
where there were irises.

## THE VOICE ON THE OTHER END OF THE LINE

The voice on the other end of the line
says nothing.  Twice.  It says nothing.

The phone breathes, deeply.  Twice.
Doing exercises.  Heavy breathing.

No one answers when the phone rings.
Twice.  It is silent in the abbatoir.

A door opens and closes.  Twice.
Dust rustles on the window.

A man shot through the temple falls.
Twice.  Dry blood on the widowed carpet.

A woman sighs into her glass of white wine.
Twice.  Ice forms on the telephone cable.

Ice slides through the doorway.  Twice.
There is no warmth in the closet.

A dog dies of heartworms.  Horribly.
Twice.  Answer the telephone.  Breathing.

ON WRITING

i.
The prisoner inside
demands apprehension.

ii.
The hand does not prevent
the mind from committing
poetry.

iii.
These poems are the children
of all poets in all times.

iv.
These poems lose weight.
They are hungry.

v.
These poems will multiply.
They will believe in genocide.

vi.
These poems are patriotic.
They will discover treason.

vii.
These poems go to war.
They believe in revolution.

viii.
These poems will stop madness.
They do not believe in treatment.

ix.
These poems will kill.
They are the ultimate graffiti.

## ON FINDING A POEM UNDERNEATH THE BED

Quite by accident, I
have found this poem
lying underneath the bed.

It is a strange bed, of
course, not mine, for
I am in a house of
strangers.

It is not my poem, of
course, it is in a strange
hand, saying things alien
to me.

It is a love poem, of
course, and a poem
about death.  It is
very old.  It
is dying.
It appears to have been
written before the turn
of the century.  The lines of ink
have faded, are now barely
legible.  The paper cracks
beneath the slight press
of my fingers.  It is now broken
into three pieces.

One piece of the poem is about
love, one, about death; the third
about Indians,
about the earth, about hate

and territory.  It is a poem
written around America
and the universe of love
and hate and death
that writes all poetry.

I am prepared to spend
some years of my life
reading these poems, writing
out of them, living them, wanting
to find the hand that set them
down on paper.

PART TWO

KILL, DIE, LIVE
*for Ron Dunham*

The buck has not hurt your life.
He does not know you have one.
He forages, when there is underbrush.
He does not pillage or rape or vandalize.
He comes into your field of vision—
an innocent, a stranger
who has learned to keep a head-high
lookout for sunlight glinting
from rifle sights, to hear the sudden
crack of branches and weeds under human feet.
He is a proud buck, this one; six points
like a defiant diadem on his head.
He freezes, becomes a courtly prince
watching and waiting for his king to motion him forward
to the sharp dull throne of blood.
If you are close enough to see his eye
your finger pulses on the trigger,
your hand falters on the bow.
You see the flow of life in him
You sense the dignity of his life,
the disorder of your own.

Hunting is different—different
from everything you believe, because you believe
in life and you revere the living.
Pulling the trigger, watching the bullet
smash away brown eyes, watching the great crown
hurtle backward, seeing the lovely brown legs
working at the air as though running, bounding
away from you.  He dies.  And you are left
with the butcher's work you came for.
                              The icy morning

seems colder, the air is electric,
sparks connect your glove and your nose
when you reach to wipe the drool away.

You walk slowly, like a man who has just heard
that a friend is dead.  You bend down and touch
the steaming carcass.  You recoil
as the last, great heave of air breaks from him.

How different it is.  How unlike
standing before the white, brightly-lighted,
semi-sterile, overflowing counters of cuts of beef,
and pork and veal in the supermarket,
where the obedient lieutenants
of the A and P, the Safeway, Kroger's and Grand Union
have committed all your murders for you,
leaving your hands, like Himmler's and the Chiefs
of Staff in the Pentagon, the President's,
unbloodied, your mind and stomach
undisturbed.

# THE NEWS ABOUT WEISSMULLER

> (From an A.P. radio bulletin, Sunday, the
> 22nd of December, 1973: *'From Las Vegas
> comes word that Johnny Weissmuller, for-
> mer Olympic swimming star and the screen's
> most famous Tarzan, has been hospitalized
> after a fall in Caesar's Palace, where he
> was employed as . . .'*)

After a fall?  None of that.
All that grace.  The body that fell like wind
from the sky.  Stark lines like a panther
calling the elephants to come and tramp upon
the evil whites and their blackmen-whores,
giving the jungle back to beasts and good men.
Captured, at times, but freed by animal guile,
and, all the while, erect, calm, certain to stand,
an obelisk, among animals and men.
And never          fall.

> (From an A.P. radio bulletin, Monday, the
> 23rd of December, 1973: *'Doctors at
> Southern Nevada Hospital said tonight
> that former Olympic swimming star Johnny
> Weissmuller has suffered a severe heart
> attack.  The screen's most famous Tarzan
> is listed in critical . . .'*)

We were the Riders of the Purple Sage.
You were King of the Jungle.
We rode hard to beat the sunset,
racing the herd to night camp.
You ran with the herd, all golden grace,
swinging from vines.

Our mounts foamed at mouth and saddle.
There were sores on our asses at the end of the day.
Your loins never perspired.
The hide at your privates stayed perfectly in place.
You found Jane in the Jungle.
We found Nothing at the Campfire.
She bore you a son.
We were childless.
We rode into the sunset, became machines.
You built swimming pools, became legend.

We are in the sunset.
You are in Las Vegas.
We die without notice.
You are an hourly bulletin
that you are the former Olympic champ
who played Tarzan of the Apes.
And when we think of this,
Mark Spitz becomes a shadow of a backstroke,
holding his Schick shaver in his hand.

And you are, once again, there in the vines,
standing with Maureen and Johnny and Cheetah,
watching the tigers, the elephants and the rhinos
drive the greed of white men from the world
you make noble in monosyllables.

If you *are* dying—and you may be—
I hope they do not hitch you up with wires
and plastic tubes or pump you full of false life
or break your great swimmer's heart with years
of vegetation.  Let them     let you     let go
of life, as you did vines,
trumpeting your vigor and your honesty
with the good grace of savages,

full, fine, plunging into the thick of death
as you did life.
Not as a sign of something passed
or passing, but as the man we once knew, in darkness,
who gave us, in our childhood, something like mystery,

like    Light.

# ISADORA, DANCING

i.

She was like Light
spilling across a courtyard
falling crosswise through space
upon a stage
whose only people were the veils of aftermath.
She was — oh, God — she was the breath
that comes with birth,
the rasping file of old will, dying.

She changed the world
the style of dress
the form of fashion

the norm . . .

ii.

'I was one of her first students
there were six of us
i was with her *seventeen years*
i knew her as no one else
knew her
she was the only one who understood
the human body
how it should move
what it should do

in ballet, you know, they use their hands
and their feet and they do nothing with the torso
nothing with most of their bodies

it was a time when women were not supposed to show
their thighs

when it was immoral for women to be seen in public
without shoes

she changed all that
because she knew that the spirit must be free
or man could not be
anything

and the spirit was the Dance!

Now they are making movies
films! sensational! filled with dirt!
filth to sell tickets!

my friend George Cukor went to her
(that girl!) and said
you *must* have Anna!
Anna is the only one who knew!
Anna is the only one.

But she took some middle-aged housewife
from Vienna
who could never have studied with anyone
except Elizabeth!

and they made the children move like oxen

here!     here!
look at their legs,
how they plod about even when they are running!

they made her a whore,
that's what they've done!
a whore!

and she was not!

she was          *Isadora!*

iii.

           From the shopping bag
clutched between her legs
clippings erupt
printed ashes across my desk
the fire of half-forgotten lava
spills into my hands
and burns,
possessive as the memory
of
    Isadora
        dancing
            dancing
                dancing . . .

# A ROOM

*. . . I have the feeling that I shall go mad and*
*cannot go on any longer in these terrible times.*
*I hear voices and cannot concentrate on my work.*
*I have fought against it, but cannot fight any longer . . .*

Was it the Time, Virginia?
Or was it only echoes of the day
When God closed both his hands
Around our middle body and portrayed us human?
That matter which resolved into the earth was dust
And Man, through dust, became
Reflected fire.  The name
For it is Time.  But *was* it the Time?

Some feeling that insinuates into the mind
And vocally intrudes upon the levelled mirror.
Some nature running crosswise, countered clocks
Of fair despair and gnawing recognition.
Some insolence of officers around the continent
Whose lips speak ancient aliens of sound
In vast omnipotence of air.  Some circled
Cry of doves in anarchistic arcs above the flue
Where carcass hangs like drying clothes.
A strutting paperhanger fell through paper floors
And struck a semblance of a symbol on the wall
Where blood ran like a tapestry into the floor.
The mores cluttered our abysmal libraries,
Slew the clerk who checked out Joyce
And fell like clustered olives in the pit of blind
Unsounded minds.  Where tricks of our mentality
Grew in parasitic fright, the host disparaged us
And took our minds away from politics
Turned backward to dessert and proper forks and spoons.

And all about the fortress of this island
Was the unknown, great, predictable desire:
Immense in trembling
Where the silence flew into the rock
No sirens sang nor shoreboys waited for the winging ship
To dock; no callers came and waited for the ending journey
Or the dying day.
White rock portrays . . . serenity, in part,
And virgin virtues fall within the mind
To block a pathway for the lesser birds.
And from this emptiness of sound
Came growing harshness; deep, unsleeping
Fear of fright.  These particulars of fate
Distend the thoughtful brow into commissioned anger,
And, at last, defeat, despair.

   ——— The feeling, when it came,
      Was only discontent, malaise;
      The kind of fretful searching one does
      For the right word or the proper phrase.
      And little more.  Yet, once it had begun
      There was no keeping out the deadening
      Of cartilage, the rotting flesh,
      The stripping, bleeding wound.

  ——— *I shall go mad* and not remember how the walls behaved
    Before the room began its dancing
    Or the house stood still.
    *Go mad* and fall down endless steps to where the moss in bloom
    Incenses every movement with its terrible tears.
    *Go mad* and walk the sightless hedge down to the sea and beach
    To where the gulls lie only a little further, out of reach.
    *Go mad* and tear my fleshy fingers bare.
    *Go mad* and feel the need to kill.  To kill.
    The house stood still.  And stands.  Still stands.
    The house stands still.

*44*

——— If I told you: Cannot go on.
Your sympathy would lie to me
And say: Of course.
And so I would.
And so I write it now, instead
And cannot speak.
The walls, each time I say aloud:
I cannot concentrate!
Smile down benignly, seem to wait
And hover on my shoulder, listening.

——— Another thing:
I heard him speak last night.
A tragic voice it was, hard with some peculiar scent
Of foreign words and lines. The guttural oblique
Before my eyes intended to be kind, I'm sure,
And yet was not. Goethe? In my sleep, I thought perhaps
It might have been. Yet when I woke and listened,
Knew it could not be.
Sounded somehow like that man who sold us artichokes
Or chou-fleur.
I'd heard the voice before . . .

——— So, there it is. It was. The feeling.
And the voices in the room beside me as I worked
Not saying what they meant; no, not at all.
And how the feeling grew until I felt there
Was no more—could not go on.
To press the ears, refuse to listen
Was not quite enough.
The paper rustled and disturbed the pen.
I knew that they were there.

——— Now, I write this. A gesture of finality
And mystery as old as God and this child Man.

The words are little words of little worth
To mark the riverpath on which I ran.

So was it, down the sucking pool of thought
Took to the fishes and the hooks unending,
Through the pulsebeat of the stream
And man's life, gone?  What voices
When you sank below your hair
Called after you or under you,
To Where?  And, finished with the word,
Too soon, did this stream punctuate
Your breath as proper souls
Or were there symbols of infinity?

Sunk to the bottom where the sands began their climb
About your body, through the grey lips —
Was it the Time?

IGNORING WHITMAN

Some of them remembered.
Years afterward, there were letters,
Written in the tight, cramped script
of farm boys who had never known
the written word.
                    Saying:
'You were father to me
when I had no father
and I can still call up to memory
your hands
as they brushed back my hair
that night the shells hit our bivouac.
It was like a dream,
some kind of prayer to me
for all the noise of death
around me stopped
and I could hear my mother, praying at supper,
for our bread, and our salvation.'

And some of them were letters,
pain-drawn, filled with prayer,
from mothers who had caught
the cadence of the dying.

'You will not remember
my son Phillip
for he was one of many,
I am told,
for whom you were
the last breath of humanity.

'He wrote me once, before he died,
in some strange final nurse's hand

that you were there
when he had doubted most.  When, in the night,
he cried and you had damped the tears.
How you stayed and comforted his heart.
That your strong hand had grasped his own
and pulled him back to one last hope
before the end.

'I write you, now,
as Phillip's mother,
as one who cannot know
what force within you made you
strong enough to count the minutes of that night;
to say to you that you are blessed
and that my son,
dead these months,
could say to me in his last hours,
        'I love you, now
          as I had not known I could
          for I have found that men can find
          themselves only when
          they have seen the pure
          and selfless love of other men.'

'I shall not ever see you,
for you are in a world apart from mine.
I should not know what words to speak
should we meet.
                But please do know
that in those final words,
I saw my son as I had not before.
And, knowing him, as I do now,
I now know you.
                Go, good man,
and safely work.  There are many,
some dead, some living, who should know of you.

IF?
*for Sam McDowell*

It would have been enough, after all,
to be a common drunk. (There are no
common drunks.) Could have been
a dishwasher, a short order cook,
a men's clothing store clerk.
Could have been a farmhand,
a trucker, a waiter, a spray painter,
a carpenter.  Could have said:  This is all
there is to it; why try for something more?
Could have said:  fuck it, don't care
about anything but number one.
Each drunk has a separate story,
something unusual. (There are no unique
stories, sober or drunk.) But, if you listen,
they do not sound the same.  Most of it has to do with love,
the straining lack of it.  Loneliness (there is no such
thing as being alone; there are too many echoes
of washing dishes, frying 60 orders of eggs—over easy,
sunny-side up, basted, soft, hard), selling bad shirts
and rotten shoes to men who can't afford
even the badness or the rottenness;
plowing a field of black dirt, watching
the dust whip across the ground
that once grew corn or wheat and now grows nothing
but stubble; orders for hamburgers, spiked high
on the shelf above the cook's counter by the whip-legged
blond from Davis City; Adam and Eve on a raft; watching the red
of the primer coat give way to olive drab;
spackling the phony foliage on the side of the generators
or tank plates; feeling the grain of good wood
on your fingers, knowing, at last, the grain cannot last.
The grain is wrong.  As soon as the knife bites into it,

the wood will split.
                    The past will not endure.
The chips will fire and turn to ashes.  They will be
mixed with the dirt, plowed under.  The wind will whip
about the furrows, along the narrow ridges;
the seeds will be left for crows to pick.
And there will be no grain.

Grain, Wood grain.  Against the grain.  Booze.

Grain.  Could have been.
Could have been enough.

MEMORIAL

i.

After he was gone, she left the bed
as it had been.  Unmade, crumpled
in the corner of the dim room, it stood
day upon night as the stalled time
she knew would not come again.

At night, often, on weekends, in mid-day
she would lie on it, fondling the folds
of sheet, the rough, wool-scratch
of his blanket.  She slept between
the sheets, pulling them tight about
her breasts, stretching them between her thighs,
feeling again the hard tensions
of his body, the calm, clothlike
tenderness of his hands across her back,
her arms and breasts as he pressed
into her.  His pillow became his buttocks,
clenched in her cracked fingers, pulled
against her, upon her, into her.  She sucked
her breath in, gasping for air, greedy
in her want, her need to give, to be taken
from this bed down into the coral reef
and tunnelled sand.  In the quiet
she breathed in the shot, remembered
sweat, the places where the sheet
had caught between his legs, the light
brown stain left by his anus
when he sat heavily upon the bed
after his shower.
                    She smoothed the thin
cotton with her fingertips, remembering
again the way the hair had shone, light,

shot through with its own light,
on the dark-tanned skin; the small
universe of his navel, turned in
upon itself.


ii.
In time, her sister came,
questioning the house,
the way it looked,
the bed.
          "These sheets are filthy,"
she said.  "You'll die of plague
or ague.  You cannot live like this."


iii.
She knew her sister's
fear of dirt.  And the root
of dirt—the human body.

She remembered her sister
screaming in the back room
of the big house
the night of her wedding.


iv.
She took the sheets
from the bed
with the gentle hands
of a woman oiling a baby,
lifting them
as she might
a fevered child.

She folded them in upon themselves,
smoothing them down,

patting them, making them neat, in squares.

Then she laid them, with great care,
in the back of the bottom bureau drawer.

v.
But each night, and, often,
in mid-day, she opened the drawer,
removing them, holding them to her cheek,
caressing them, breathing into them,
and, in return, sucking from them,
the sharp, cut flesh of her dreams.

vi.
Her sister visited less often.
Those friends she had, moved
out of town, or died.
She did not attend the services,
she sent no flowers.
She was seen less and less
at the local store.
She had her phone removed,
with instructions that the wire
was to be cut and taken
from the pole outside her home.

vii.
In winter, when the snow
drifted above the highway
and workmen with orange
tractors threw themselves
relentlessly against the midwest cold,
they opened a narrow pathway to her door,
finding her alone, lying on her bed,
clutching the dull grey sheets
between her hands like a book of common prayer.

viii.
A note on the kitchen table,
frozen to the oil cloth,
with its fading design of red
apples and strawberries,
read:

      "Sister:

      I want Tom's sheets

      put in my casket with me

      when you bury me."

ix.
Her sister came, after Barnes,
the funeral director, had taken
her from the house.  She read
the note, distastefully.

But she knew she could not deny
voices from the grave.
She took the sheets from the corner
of the bed and boiled them
for an hour in the 18-quart canner
on the wood stove.

x.
At the funeral home
she placed the sheets,
white and starched and folded,
at her sister's side.

The old men and women mourners
who passed the coffin at the viewing
noticed little more than the color
of her skin, the mottle of her hair,
the way her hands were folded.

Only her sister knew that she
had washed all signs of life
out of her death.

# PART THREE

# FIFTEEN STEPS FOR ULTIMATE SURVIVAL: GROUND ZERO

**One**

Do not discover sex.

> Washington, D.C. (AP) The U.S. Bureau of Census said today that the population of the nation will surpass 300 million by the year 1999.

**Two**

Do not discover fire.

> Boulder, Colo. (UPI) At least 210 children died tonight in the flaming holocaust of a Colorado juvenile home. Authorities said the flames were fed by highly flammable carpeting and drapes in the 97-year-old building.

**Three**

Do not discover fire.

> *(Special to The News)*
>
> Providence—A nine-year-old boy was charged today with dousing his paralyzed baby sister in kerosene and setting a match to her.
>
> Neighbors said they became aware of the tragedy when . . .

**Four**

Do not discover fire.

> Los Angeles (UPI) The Environmental Protective Agency warned today that fumes from motor vehicles will force the closing of all major highways and the construction of barricades on all inner city streets within a week.
>
> Commissioner Arnold Karp told

newsmen at an emergency press conference: "The internal combustion engine has . . .

### Five

Do not discover fire.

Kiska (Reuters) Underground tests conducted Monday by the Atomic Energy Commission today apparently created a chain reaction, setting off three formerly lifeless volcanoes. By nightfall the entire Ryukyus Islands and the southernmost tip of Japan were reportedly obliterated by molten lava.

Light from the reactivated volcanoes' fires could be seen from both Attu and Kiska thousands of miles away. It was believed to be the worst natural disaster since Krakatao.

### Six

Do not invent the wheel.

Washington (AP) The National Safety Council said today that 78,613 persons lost their lives in motor vehicle accidents last year. It was the worst year on record, according to . . .

### Seven

Do not discover alcohol.

. . . who said that no less than 78 percent of reported accidents involved drunken drivers.

### Eight

Do not invent papyrus.

*(The New York Times Service)*

Washington—Pentagon officials were embarrassed today by columnist Jack Anderson's report that more than 62 billion tons of paper had been accumulated during the Vietnam war.

**Nine**
Do not invent papyrus.

Meanwhile, psychiatrist Joel Waldheim said that the Vietnam war created a "paper block" for officials and became impossible of solution. Massive quantities of memos between the Pentagon, the White House, the CIA, the Congress and Saigon went unread and unheeded, Waldheim said. He attributed this to the "corporate incapacity of the human mind to absorb . . ."

**Ten**
Do not invent the telephone.

*(from Scientific American)*

Massive failure of circuitry in the U.S. telecommunications system in 1973 was attributed this year to "total and inept usage of microwave tower equipment and computerization."

A report filed with the Interstate Commerce Commission and the Committee on Interstate Commerce in the U.S. House of Representatives charged, in part, that the nation is "headed back to the days of the five-party line and the hand crank telephone instrument."

**Eleven**

Do not invent the telephone.

The head of a special commission investigating a 2600-percent increase in mental hospital commitments in Manhattan in 1973 told the Times today that "all or nearly all of the cases showing no pre-history of emotional disturbance which have entered hospital wards this year are victims of the mechanical failure of the New York telephone system."

Dr. Kraus Wicken, dean of psychiatric studies at Johns Hopkins, reported that 172,618 patients now under treatment for the first time had complained of "massive and cumulative frustration" in dealing with New York Bell.

**Twelve**

Do not invent the telephone.

Provo (UPI)  Allen Baker, 42, was charged today with murder in the death of Mountain Bell official Harold Werkis.

Attorneys for Baker said the owner of a local antique shop became enraged when his repeated efforts to correct an erroneous telephone bill went unheeded by Werkis and other Bell employees.

Carl Baker (no relation) said his client received a bill in the amount of $988.88 last March. The bill listed long distance calls to Montevideo, Osaka, San Luis Obispo and other

exotic locations unknown to the de-
fendant.

## Thirteen
Do not invent the telephone.

Minneapolis (AP) Mary LaBerge
filed suit in Federal Court here today
charging that the Bell Telephone
Company had caused her "grievous
and irreparable mental and emo-
tional harm" through a "series of un-
solicited calls from real estate brok-
ers, subscription salesmen and out-
right crooks."

In addition to seeking a sum of
$700,000 in damages, Ms. LaBerge
asked the court to order the phone
company to "immediately remove
from our premises any and all instru-
ments or other equipment alleged to
belong to the company."

## Fourteen
Do not invent the
printing press.

Washington (UPI)  The United
States toDAY declared wxcjil on the
Sovvvv xiion, charging infringement
of terpodiurjtl jdiurkrklogp   lod,lfo
. .; a nxndnhur ikikbhkodm. Presi-
aokl Niiin tooold a somber and silent
jint sssion othe joint sesiiin of the
HOuse adn Snate that xjhhehdhdyur
jdjirikgolsllldkkfjklsjkkff

reset

the qwck brnow xof jped
ovvvvvvv

**Fifteen**

Do not invent the telephone.

*(The New York Times Service)*
Presidential adviser A. K. Morrissey today blamed the outbreak of World War III on the direct dialing system.

more to come to come

# ON THE RAPID TRANSMISSION OF BAD NEWS

Call me any
time.  I am used to getting
bad news
on the phone.

Death travels so fast
by area code
and seven-digit direct
dialing
marital breakups
quarrels   suicides   and divorce
even premature
pregnancies
followed by the still born
seem to flash like
sheet lightning
through the air
into my ear

The ringing phone
scars the night
flesh and sound sleep
once asunder
calls me back to dreams
of death, divorce
and argument
of the blue face
of the baby I shall never know

Call me any
time   day   night   eternity
I grow accustomed to this corporate
accumulation of

bad news

ON BEING / HUMAN / BEING ON

**On Birth**
Wail.  Flail the air with your fists.
Cry out against it. You did not ask
for this madness.

**On Love**
Learn early that you can live
without it, if you do not care
for life.

**On Food**
The things that are not
really good for you
are the things you do not like.

**On Sex**
Try not to see more in it
while it's happening
than you will recognize
in the mirror next morning.

**On Need**
Try not to need too much.
What you really need is
to be needed.

**On Death**
It is the one thing
you cannot complain about
tomorrow.

**On Reincarnation**
Try not to make
the same mistake
again.

**On Androgyny**
Where beauty is,
beauty lives.
We are all/one.

**On Whitman**
He opened the grass.
Wind caught his semen.
A thousand poets were born.

**On Ego**
Half a cup
will be
plenty.

**On Teaching**
Learning that teaching
is learning
is teaching.

**On Marriage**
Flail the air with your fists. Wail!
Cry out against it. You need not ask
for this madness.

EVERYTHING IN ITS PLACE
*for Nancy Hanks*


For those of you who have never seen
my desk, let me describe it.  It is
officially recognized as a landmark
of our office, for nearly all who visit
are ushered to my door to gaze at its
complexity.  Hundreds have been led
from it murmuring, with some distaste,
of chaos, disaster and confusion.

Now, let me say, in its defense
that it happens by no accident
that my desk is as it is.  It is
not an island, to be sure.  It is part
of the real world.  And it reflects
that world with marked and, some would say,
remarkable acuity.  When, let us posit,
there is war, my desk takes sides, sets
up its battle-lines, its own perimeters;
engages in hand-to-hand combat with
the chairs, the floor, the walls.
It is, invariably, the victor.

My desk has been known to take a manic
mood, rattling about with gaiety
and abandon; most notably at Halloween
and on Wallace Stevens' birthday.  It can
become depressed, as when the latest purist
committee denies admission to Ezra Pound
or it receives the latest issue of American PEN,
a magazine of rejects.  On at least one occasion,
when it stormed outside, it even rained.

My desk has character.  It has dignity,
very like that one associates with elderly
drunken ladies who are determined to pronounce
their words correctly.  More often than not
it loses its temper when strangers ferret
about in it searching for this or that lost
document.  It does not suffer fools gladly.
It sustains me, and that is quite enough of
foolishness for any desk.  It catches cold
in Summer, for, like its owner,
it hates conditioned air.

It is a monolith, a structure from pre-
history, a totem for those who worship
the mind, who love the clutter of ideas.
It is an ocean; its waves are white-flecked
letters filled with poems from small children
in midwestern schools; its breakers are books
of poetry and prose, from strangers and friends;
they wash over me as I lie in my chair waiting
for moonrise.  Since I do not take vacations
it is my solace, my spiritual sinkhole,
my surrogate beach.

It is an echo of my earliest times, when
we saved everything; a polaroid of my mind;
a grotto of other times.  My grandmother,
who led a life disordered by her own demands
for order, once had a motto:  A place for
everything, everything in its place.  And yet
the only place she ever owned was bought
and paid for by her daughter and her son-
in-law after she was dead.  And so, my desk
is my place, my tomb and my escarpment.
And it is orderly, no matter what wry comments
may be made.

Knowing it, as you now do, do you wonder
that people pause in awe of it?  Do you doubt
that they fear to touch it, knowing as they do
that the slightest brush among its papers
may enrage it, may cause it to reach into them
and submerge them in its pulls and tides,
carry them downward beneath the gulls and guppies
to the dark hooks of the coral, breaking them,
flying into their lungs like wet angels
until they are finally, mercifully drowned?

PART FOUR

VILLAGE DYING

There are always hints of resurrection.
Death bites the flesh and pulls away
The breath, sucking the muscle,
Snapping the tendons of the meat.
They have watched the gooks die on TV,
Seen the Jews and Arabs maim each other;
They hear late reports of bombing by the IRA.
And they remain calm, watching the monster
Ocean from their windows.  Nothing about
These things is new, requires comment.
That is a world of blood and slaughter
Where animals become men only by accident.
Their fathers were fishers, their mothers, weavers.
They do odd jobs, work on the highway,
Drive assassinated Chevies from the white man's
Boneyard.  Their children leave them,
Those who survive, go to Seattle, find Spirit
In bottles.  The others will stay here with ghosts
Of dead gooks flickering before them on the screen
Of their existence, dying in place, walking
Ever more slowly, looking far into the ocean,
Counting Death as you might count your change.

AMERICAN JUSTICE

The Clallam sits at a table
in the bar, waiting for his son
to bring him a glass of tokay
wine.  His great-grandfather
was a chief.  They were a peaceful
nation.  They loved this rain-soaked
battered country.  He loves
it still.  He sips the wine.  Like
other Indians over 40 in the bar
he keeps his eyes down, steady,
on the table, tracing
some invisible design.
The bartender is half-Quilieute.
He takes food stamps
for the wine, trading them later
to the grocer next door.
Ten years ago he went to jail
for killing a white man in self-defense.
He cannot leave it, now,
no matter where he goes.
He stays here, his own jailer,
keeper, warden, carrying his cell
about him like the skin of sheep.
The television flickers
with the latest news of Watergate.
The president of the United States
is on the screen.  "Don't worry,"
the bartender says.  "There's one guilty
son of a bitch who'll never serve time."

# FLIGHT TO ATLANTA FROM COLUMBIA, S.C.

The young black boy next to me is strapped
tightly to his seat.  He has never flown
before.  We taxi out on the runway.
"Do you know how to get more air?"
he asks.  I adjust the nozzles overhead
Cold air spurts down on sweat.
He grins and says "I'm goin' to Seattle.
Goin' to the Army.  I tole my momma
I wouldn't see her for two three years or more."
His eyes dart right as the rubber-metal
beast lurches from the ground. The sound
of landing gear hoisted causes him to jump,
large, dark eyes pressed outward.
"It's just the wheels coming up," I say,
"nothing to worry about.  It's okay."
"Sure," he says.  "I figured." He smiles
and lights up the second the "No Smoking"
sign goes out.  The dark dung smell of
the Camel fills the air.  "I tole my momma
I couldn't call or write her till I got
settled down at Fort Lewis," he says.
When we land at Atlanta, he asks the flight
attendant how to get to a pay telephone.

# FLIGHT FROM ATLANTA TO DALLAS/FORT WORTH

It's a 747.  Great pterodactyl of Boeing
technology and greed.  I settle
into seat number 29H.  The grey man
in the grey suit next to me asks me
to put his coat in the locker overhead.
His voice is a guttered whisper,
something left from a deeper time.
Halfway to Dallas, after six cigarets
and two bourbons and branch water,
he says: "I suppose you're wondering
why I talk this way." I nod, my mouth
full of smoke and scotch.
"I had cancer of the throat
eight years ago.  They went in
and cut it out.  Never come back.
I feel great, got a good body.
Not bad for 63." He lights another Camel,
leans forward to catch the blue-blonde
stewardess on her way by.  "How about
another bourbon and water?" "Just be
patient, sir," she says.  "We'll be comin'
right back your way, again."

## FLIGHT TO AUSTIN FROM DALLAS/FORT WORTH

The color-coded (green) shuttle
takes me from Delta to Braniff
where the color-coded flight
attendant (purple) gives me a boarding
pass to the 727 where the color-
coded stewardess (red, blue, ashen blonde)
tears off part of it and sends me to
my color-coded (yellow) seat on the aisle
in the smoking section, next to a
girl who is with her boy-friend,
who is also, color-coded.

SOME SENSE OF THE PAST,
SOME KNOWLEDGE OF THE PRESENT
*for Jim McGrath*

i.

Fire comes
and fades

ice forms
and runs away

rocks fall
breaking apart

dust rises
with your footsteps
as you walk away

nothing is
or will be
as it was
or
as it is

fire
dust
rain
clouds of love
or of despair
rock
rim rock
dust clouds
from the year before

tomorrow

ii.
Look at the grey bricks carefully
and you will see the dead strands
of another life,
of families whose births and deaths
were mud and mortar for this ruin
Raël    Romero    Sanchez

just the dead trees
just the dying wind
were here and here remain

stones in the corner of the room
speak of the years of dry season

the dust of the dirt floor
rising with each step
(as you walk away)
rising  rising  rising
calling like signals
out of their lives
through the corridors of our own

the shattered bits of glass
green gleanings of another dream
dulled by biting sun
lie in their wind-built nests
yielding to human fingers
grudgingly

iii.
Prisms of the earth
shifting ochre
in the vaulted rim of rock
above this roofless house

all the colors
all the tremors of the earth
all the sadness   triumph   challenge
change and challenge
victory


just the dry grass   growing on the cliffside
just the cactus   proud pre-eminent dustlike
and enduring
just the small smells of the earth   and sky
just the clouds and the people of the clouds
and the spirit of the dark clouds
hanging on the rim of this horizon
here to remind us of


Sanchez     Romero     and     Raël


iv.
This is a country of hawks and dead birds
sheep carcasses turned brown in wind and wearing
        rain
whose shadows   birdlike   skim across
        the countries of our consciousness
causing contradiction   questioning   and pain
whose dark hills hold us as they pinion
        our arms   and minds
within this shining valley


v.
We have been here before, here in this grey
        abandoned room
.this doorframe, this dim adobe reckoning of homes
a thousand years ago.  Have been here, lived
            here, heard
the wind-psalm of a thousand days

seen the fire blaze   seen the dry wood eaten
        by the flame

We have been here and remained here
with    Raël    and    Sanchez    and    Romero
with their children and their dying animals
with the shadows of their living
and the lightning stillness
of their passing
into these hills and streams
into the soul of earth    the clouds of prayer
incantations
and fulfillment
into the will that will become
survival.

# LETTER DICTATED ON HORSEBACK

You may not remember me.
Time being what it is
just as I forgot your name
so you with mine.
Yet some part of you remembers
being rock and river; storm and calm;
nature and force and peace; forgetfulness.
I am the man
who rode into the wind
whose dark hair
you remember
flying like the horse's mane
whose lean thighs
clenched the roan ribs
and the belly
whose voice
died in the hills
on the other side of Casper.

A PASSAGE TO SHERIDAN

There is no light like this
anywhere on earth — pure light
caught in grand expansive cradles
in the foothills
(whose sooty flecks of dark light
flow like sleeping prehistoric beings
in the shadows of the unseen Big Horns).

Light unlike the light of sun
(or moon or stars)
exploded energy from a giant handful
of the purple earth.

Across the foothills
a storm is rising
white bristling with the fury
and the echo of the world's first wind

Breaking upon us
our pitiable 3,000 pounds
of steel, aluminum and chrome
thrashes upon the highway
as a caged beast
or a trapped bird
or a trout caught in the last deep spasm
of existence

Now in the storm
in the center of this universe
of demonic beauty
and its traceless calm

we come to Sheridan

## RIDING TO RICHMOND ON SATURDAY MORNING

The Trailways bus depot in
Washington, D.C.
smells of vomit
and spilled wine.

At 7:30
the thick black voice
of the attendant
announces bus-now-loading-
on-platform-3-for-
Spring-field-Fred-
ericksburg-Rich-
mond&Wil-ming-
ton.  A black policeman
raises a long black
stick and strikes a black
bum in the groin.  He falls
off the bench where he has been
sleeping and spins on the floor
like a black Sonja Henie
on ice.  I step toward
him but the black policeman
pounds his stick in the palm
of his hand, looking at me.

I get on board the bus
to Richmond.


●


At Springfield a black woman with a small baby
and two suitcases gets on
the bus, bumps her way to the back

where you can smoke.
I get up and help her put the bags
in the rack above the seats.
She smiles; has one tooth missing
in the front.

The white man sitting behind me stares
as I sit down.  And quickly spits
in the aisle.  The baby laughs.


●


At Fredericksburg
a white man with a thick waist
and thick arms sits down
in the seat beside me.  He wheezes
when he breathes.  He breathes
on me.  In my ear.  On my hand
when I light his cigaret.

Smoke three packs a day.  Smoked
all my life.  Got started
when I was ten.  Never seen no need
to quit it.  Gonna die anyhow.
'Tain't your lungs its gonna be
your liver.  My old lady
tried to get me to stop.  Said
it was a filthy habit.  Then she got
to know me better'n found out what
filthy habits kin really be.
Got her divorce five years ago.
Don' see her much.  But I got custody
rights on my boy every other weekend.
Y'otta see 'im.  Big little bugger.
Bigger'n me when I was his age.

Got arms like a sidea beef'n a cock
like a sledgehammer.  Dam kid busted
me right in the mouth onct when we was
rasslin', nen he just stood back and laughed
he thought that was the damnedest funniest goddam
thing he ever did see, me standin' there in the bathroom
tryin'ta stanch the blood.  Coulden help laughin'
muhself when its all over.

My daddy, now he was somethin'.  He was jus' like me
fuck anything in sight long as it had skirts.
Got hisself arrested twice on F and B
and even did some time in county jail.
Died a year ago.  Doc said it was cancer.
But they din cut him open or nothin.
Last five year or so of his life he walked
real funny, liftin his foot up high afore
he put it down, shakin a lot, he tole me din care if he
live or die coz he couldn't get it up no more.  Laughed
like a hyena when he said it, though, so's you never
knew whether he meant it or not.

See this thing here on my lip?  'at's where the boy
smacked into me.  Don' know why but ever six months or so
it sort of swells up and gets purple,
nen it goes away.


●


The Richmond Trailways depot
is mostly black.
A white cab driver
picks me up
and drives down Broad
to Jefferson.

He warns me that cab rates have
gone up the week before and lots
of folks don't like it.  Says
he don't like it either
but it may be good coz
it keeps some folks from takin
cabs you don' want to pick up anyway.


●


We pass a plaque on a house
lived in by the Surgeon General
of the Confederate Army.

At the Jefferson Hotel
an old black man who is hard of hearing
is yelling into a telephone
at a cab dispatcher
who is very likely not.

The great marble columns of the old hotel
shine luminously in the twilight lobby.
The dim light from the chandeliers
and their hundred crystals
softens the wine of the carpet
on the enormous stairs.


●


At lunch we are entertained
by eight young ladies from local schools.
They are dressed in long gowns.
There are six black ladies and two white ones.
They are conducted by a young white lady
who is introduced by a young white lady

who, in turn, has been introduced
by a middle-aged white matron.

On a cue from their conductor
the eight young ladies
reach forward in unison
and bring their harps into position.
There are six troubador harps
and two pedal harps.

At another signal
they begin to play,
the strong, graceful young hands
blending in brown and white unison.

The music spills into the auditorium.

It is black and brown and grey and white
and yellow and mauve and, gently, beige.

They are intent upon their playing.
Their eyes dart swiftly to the conductor.
They smile, together, as their hands damp
the sound from their singing instruments.

The audience applauds them warmly.
The applause rolls like tides upon the proscenium,
breaks upon the stage.

They are in position, again.  They begin
to play.  The theme from Franco Zefferelli's
"Romeo and Juliet."  A time for us.

Their hands are like wings in the late
fall afternoon, like swallows and doves,

racing toward warmth,
fleeing from Winter.

●

The white cab driver who drives
me back to the Richmond Trailways
depot says the country has gone to hell.
Nothin's the same any more.

## THE AGENT IN ORANGE

Speed limit signs read 35 mph
30 - 40 - 45 - 35 - 50 - 55
along the two-lane asphalt and gravel road.
A sign at the side says:
Farmers' market — Closed.  Moved to new location.
Two abandoned motels.  A third, closed for the season.
A road grader moves slowly in the right lane
in a No Passing zone, with 20 cars and pickups
lined up behind.  There is a climbing lane ahead.
Then fluorescent orange markers in the road
and flashing yellow lights warn the driver
that men are working ahead.
The cars slow, their brake lights flaring.
A Chevy pickup at the head of the line
sputters to a stop and the driver begins grinding
at the engine with his starter.  The traffic stops.
There is a flagman in front of the pickup.
He holds up his hand, a uniformed marshal,
directing a parade.  The worker wears
an orange jacket, visible clearly at a hundred yards.
He walks slowly down the lane of cars,
stopping at each one.  "Accident ahead.
Nothin' serious.  VW hit one of the truck wheels.
Nobody got hurt."  When he gets to my car
it's obvious he wants to talk, so I encourage him.
He says:  "Christ I'll be glad when this summer
is over and I'll be back in school.
This construction work sucks.  You got a cigaret?
I quit two weeks ago—smoking, I mean—but once in awhile
this job gets to me.  All this fucking traffic.
Not as bad here as it is on the Interstate, though.
I got a buddy works over on 95.  He says people
are moles, can't see nor hear, either one.

We've been lucky on this job, so far.  Only a couple of serious
smash-ups, then it's generally
people goin' too fast in the first place.
Kid got killed here last week.  Young kid.
No more than 17.  Shouldn't of been driving
in the first place.  Minute I waved him on
I knew something was going to happen.
Piled head-on into a pickup loaded
with hog feed.  Took 'em about two hours
to clean off the highway.  When they finally did,
all these people keep comin' along
and slowin' down to look at the truck
and the grain and what was left of the kid's
Datsun.  State cop said the kid was dead, even though
he got thrown out of the car.  Supposed to be safer that way.
You never know.  Job like this gets to you, what with the sun.

Well, looks like they're getting ready to move.
Nice talkin' to you.  Take it easy on that curve up ahead.
Never know what's comin'.  Okay?  Back to work.  Hell, it's a job,
    anyway.
He lopes back to the asphalt spreader, picks up his orange flag, waves
    it forward.
"Move 'em out!"

# OLD MAN

"The hell with 'em," the old man says.
"They were my children
but I ain't seen 'em for 'most 20 years.
Now he's got a big office up in Hartford.
Comes over every Christmas
and spends time with her father—her family—
up in Pittsfield.  Wife's a slut.
Screwed every hot rodder an' mechanic in Hampden County
while he was off to the Navy in Korea.
Got herself knocked up an' the baby was born
a year after he left.  When he come
back she yelled an' cried an' whimpered
like a hurt dog an' he took her back.
Been livin' together ever since.
'Course he travels a good deal so God knows
who she's sleepin' with when he's gone.

When m'woman left me, after I lost my job
with the highway department, I got one letter
from them two.  Said they knowed it was gonna be hard
but they was nothin' they could do.
Sent me a letter one Christmas, one of those things
you get printed up, all full of things about their snot-nosed
kids, includin' the boy that don't belong to him.
Soon's I saw what it was, I used it to light
the fire in the cookstove an' never wrote back at all.

My girl's out to California.  Married a guy
that was teachin' at the nuthouse over in Hartford
but he took a better job, sellin' real estate
out there to the coast.  Heard from her once.
Said they'd got this big house on the ocean
and she was pregnant again.  Sent me a card—

one of those printed things—sayin' the baby had come.
Named it Mali.  Didn't say what it was, though, a boy or girl.
Ain't heard from her again.''
                          The words stopped coming.
He looked out across the field toward Granby.  The sun
settled in for a last explosion
over behind the hills.
                    The old man rubbed his hands
together, like he was washing them, making a sound
like rough sandpaper on unplaned wood.

"Winter's gonna be rough this year.
Got to get in wood enough before the cold hits.
You see that ditch they dug up there across Route 20?
First time we get rain, all hell's gonna break loose,
you mark my words.   See ya.''

Headlights make a stark parade on the two lanes of the highway.
The old man waits to cross.

INTERSTATE BLUES

There is no mystery on The Interstate.
No sudden curves with stark black
arrow warning systems, no old jalopies
making a crusade to the neighbor's farm
for the 4th of July weekend.  The six lanes
of the Interstate become four, and then are magically
two, then transformed to six again.  The headlights
in opposing lanes flick behind bushes,
always on high beam, their studiously regimented
patterns trained like lasers at your mind.  There is a maximum
and a minimum speed on this treadmill.

Do not exceed the maximum
Do not decelerate below 45
Slow traffic keep right
The signs will tell you when to turn
        When to bear right
        When to bear to left two lanes
        for the sub base and Connecticut Rte. 184
                (formerly known as the Gold Star Highway).

An occasional smashed possum in the middle
of the road, a dead cat or two, a dog,
the black flap of retread rubber
from a long-gone truck.
The trucks ride high, bearing down
and overtaking traffic from the right.
The lights just off The Interstate
say  "OPEN ALL NIGHT", "Mechanix on duty",
"GAS!  Unleaded (Reg.) 1.21/9  Premium 1.32/9"
A bilious Holiday Inn sign dominates
a shopping mall, obliterating Two Guys, Bradlees,
Mallory, Stop & Shop.

There's no mystery on The Interstate.
No sense of discovery.
It is all laid out like cadavers in pine board boxes.
If you don't know where you've been
Or where you're going
The Next sign will tell you
If you want to know.

THE BRICK WALK

*for Alexander Harvey*


The bricks have been laid neatly
with an accurate design, curving
just enough to conform to the land around the house.
Hundreds of feet, human and animal,
walk upon the bricks, pressing
them down, ever more securely,
keeping them firm, marking
their red lines and the dark dirt that
lies between.
        The bricks seem
impressed into the soil forever—
a kind of permanent crossing
between the gravel driveway
and the back porch
and the vegetable garden that bursts
in the low part of the lawn.


        In the
center of all this green abundance—
the evergeens that loom just beyond the house,
the wildflowers breaking the grey mist
of the cloudy day—the first grass
appears in the dirt cracks
between the bricks.  No arrogance
in this, at least, at first; no signal
of interest as each thin blade breaks through,
announcing its presence by the absence of great growth.


Year after year, as seasons change,
the grass grows sturdier, greener,
those human feet step on and over them,
the grass blades tremble with their weight,

and then spring back, healthy as before,
paying no attention to these invasions,
as we have given none to them.

Slowly the bricks begin to buckle,
heaving up from the pressure of roots
below.  Soon the walk appears
to become the puzzle of a drunken
bricklayer.  The design becomes a maze
of red and black and green.  Some of the bricks
crack in patterns like lightning.

The foundation of the house
sinks, slightly at first,
then noticeably from within.

The seasons change.
The brick walk has become an obstacle
course, challenging those who would visit
the back porch or the garden.

It is winter, the time of renewal.
The bricks crumble.
The grass sleeps.

## THE DOGS OF PORT TOWNSEND

They are the ultimate citizens,
the royalty of the port.  They command
no fishing boats, no tugs, no cabin
cruisers.  They have their own domain,
the kingdom of the pickup truck,
the heraldry of traffic on Water Street
belongs to them, to their existence,
the mystery of morning fog whose softness
conceals all but their noses and their ears.

Before day comes, the first light cracking
from the Cascades in the East and breaking
on the Olympics, they sit patiently
in the backs of pickups, ever attentive,
listening for the sounds of opening doors
along the streets of Port Townsend.

In the back of a Datsun
a Malamute cants an ear
toward the rooster's cry
from across the lagoon.
He is surrounded by shards of cow manure
and air-filled swirls of straw.
The Malamute watches a red Toyota
as it makes a turn into Water Street
from market on the corner.
The woman Golden in the moving truck
leans over the edge, right paw
on the side of the truck bed,
watching the Malamute cautiously, jaws open,
spittle glinting like dew in the early sun,
eyes like the yellow flashing traffic light
at the intersection.

The streets of Port Townsend
are peopled by pickups, early in the morning,
most of them from Japan.

These wheels belong to the small cadre
of the employed — at the boatyard,
the marina, the paper box mill just outside town.
Some of the dogs go with their owners
to work.  They sit in the back of their pickups
watching people pass, staring inquisitively
at other dogs, jumping out and down
now and then, to piss
on the rear wheels of another dog's truck.
They seldom bark.  Their tails thrash
at the fog, thumping against the truckbed wall,
eager for love, open to friendship,
wanting not to be alone.

You can always tell the nature of a place
by its dogs.  They know more than you do.
They feel more than you think they feel.
They have kept just enough of the mountains,
and the plains in them
to make them able to be peaceful,
even when they are drowned by this makeshift world
houses, trucks, highways, the Sea.

# PART FIVE

THE CHILDREN

How much do they know?

        Who knows how
        much they know?

How much do they feel?

        Who feels how
        much they feel?

How much do they hear?

        Who hears how
        much they hear?

How much do they care?

        Who cares how
        much they care?

Who are they?

        They are who
        they are
        there.

They only sit
and wait
and listen
as their eyes fill
up with the room
and their lips full        un-

smiling.

## THE POET'S EYE/THE EYE OF THE STORM

i.
The poems are collected from the class
and the teacher listens
as they are read, aloud,
her face a movable mask
shifting with each reference
to alcohol or rape,
beating or murder, death by auto,
suicide by cycle, cut glass
or bullet.  The faces of the children, copper
clay, brown-eyed, solemn,
crying for pain or love

— who knows the difference?

are full, direct, unwavering.

They have their silence,
each of them,

they have their silences.

Later the teacher, blond bun bobbing
like an exclamation mark in mid-sentence
asks questions poets have heard since Homer

"Why are the things they write about so morbid?"

"Why can't they see the beautiful things?"

ii.
Statistics do not lie,
the statisticians say.

(Highest suicide rate of any community its size.
More alcoholics per capita.
Greatest unemployment rate.
Fewer fathers at home.
Highest desertion rates.
More rapes (inter-racial)
More beatings (inter-racial)
Greatest number of suicides under 21.)
The most
The greatest
the most
the highest . . .

iii.
Ah, see the pretty face of suicide,
the flower of drunkenness.

The eye of the child is a poet's eye,
the poet's eye, the center of the storm.
It is the eye of the boy
whose wrist was slashed
by the dull blade of the hunting
knife, unused to skinning game,
by the broken bottle
drained of its last lapse of memory.

It is the eye of the slim Arapahoe
stretched like wire, winding in the wind
away from the sun-red
blond-blue personnel man
who sees like stone
and shakes his head
and later says

"What can you do with Injuns?
    Never keep a job, y'know.
    Get drunk.  Won't learn.
    Shiftless.  How'd I know
    He'd go out an' hang himself?"

The poet's eye makes notes
for future reference
and flickers on
to the armless, legless
Carolina boy in the veterans' hospital
the nameless product of
a nameless war

to the children of My Lai
the blood-washed huts of unknown villages
to the children of Kent
and Orangeburg and Southern U.

It may pause to celebrate
birth or personal love
some part of the earth
left still immaculate by Man.

But the poet's eye
is the conscience of the universe
the center of what is done by man to man.

It may be music
or dissonance
it may be thunder
the final, cataclysmic
confrontation of the armies of man

Yet there is unstoppable
and incredible beauty
in the fact
that one great poet
with his eye caught
without ceasing on the ugliness of man
can move a nation
stop a country
break a war
be an army
by himself.

Wind River, Wyoming
October, 1972

# TOUCHING LIVES

There is never enough time.
You begin to read their eyes
Like windows, streaked by rain.
And time closes
the windows.

They build images in the rain,
out of water, out of mist,
the fog of forgotten guns.
Their words become doors
opening in blazing wind.
Fire guts the room,
leaving black, silver-pocked wood.
Chairs are skeletons.
The room is filled with burning flesh,
the smell of charred hair.

Until there is no fire,
no time.  The doors are closing.
The windows are broken glass
and splinters.

At the center of the room,
a hollowed skull.
And we remember
                    embering.

LaPush, Washington
28 December 1975

# THE CHILDREN AT FORT WASHAKIE

i.
These dark eyes mirror
love and loneliness
the dry-cored spirit
of a past they are denied
or cannot see

      all the dances
      all the dancers
      all the songs
      all the singers

buried in the rhythmic denigration
of antiquity
drowning in the clutter
of pure white methodology

A small-boned boy
sits in the back of the four-ring semi-circle
smiles and listens
to the sound of a poet reading

these mirror eyes
cast back the rhythms
of the words
and gently dancing fingers
drum the catches of each phrase

      O, father
      my father

      drunk
      disgraced

repentant
spiteful
filled with hatred
filled with fear
caught like an antelope
in a snare
snarling for life
raging for death
slavering, thrashing at fate
damning the gods
damning Man
damning mangods and godmen
fouling the air with black clotted bloods
holding his head
above the dry grass
above the trees
above the clouds
in a defiant thrust
of final agony
sliding, groping through death
into
his own torn
immortality.

My father
O, father . . .

A stillness in the room
breath caught in the glint of this boy's eyes
mist on the mirror of
eternity

Now we are one
father    son    death    birth
birth of death

death of birth
and brother

We come to this chant
this cant-song
reconciliation

Leaving the room
ranging upon the dusty hills
drawing the dry patterns of our lives
into the mirror of the soul

      Changing
      changing

all the songs
      the singers
all the dances
      all the dancers

Father?  Father?

      O, my father . . .

ii.
No more than ten or twelve
she is ageless and without age
the irony of relentless years
hangs rusting in her eyes

Visions of slaughter
      the death of men
             and animals
the dying of the earth
the search for water

*111*

a dusty passage in the morning
to the shadows of the mountains
and still
the planting
and the harvest

still the seeking
thirsting anger of the soil

Her dark soft eyes are on me
swallow, follow me
about the room

I kneel before a boy
across the room
reading a line
about his father

and she is watching
listening, taking the roll
of one more unrecorded moment in our history

calm recorder
warm pen
in the brown hand of tomorrow

writes
and remembers.

iii.
It is a poem about the sun
And dancers of the sun
The words are grey-warm
Filled with breaking sunlight
And the break of dreams
And the dust of dancers.

She reads it solemnly
The grace of years within her
Slight body
And in the room
The Sun appears
Immaculate
Made form (out of the dew)
Made fire (out of raging sky)
Made innocence and violence
Dancing in the long soul
Of these children
Filling our hands with heat and harvest.

These words
Are the dancers of the mind
The sun and sum of our survival.

iv.
Not just what he wrote
The careful, loving way
The words came to the paper
Traveling the universe of
A barren kingdom
Tracing the progress of a boy's soul
Into morning
And mourning's aftertaste
Self-knowing.

## FOR THREE TEACHERS AT FORT WASHAKIE

i.
Someone of course said
It would be a waste of time
Teaching any child to write
Poetry.
But *Indian* children?

Now they are here in this room
Black heads bowed,
Hands flicking across the blue-lined tablets
Eyes darting for a moment
To the wall, to the tall man
In the center of the room.
The quiet simmers with the sound of pens on paper
And the gentle, curious rustle
Of paper passed to neighbors.

ii.
She is a teacher of children
Teaching with her eyes
With the gentle dancer movement of her hands
The quiet voice and sure, calm eyes
Caressing them
Holding them
Making them

Whole

iii.
He is thin, wiry
Moves with the calm grace
of a man sure of his body.

While the children write
he sits at the window
right foot on the sill.

Beneath the sun and wind-white brows
his clear slate eyes
pass over them, child to child.

At recess
since he is the coach
he urges them to make a run
around the track
and they go, dutifully,
as young colts
at the bidding of their bursting energy.

We talk
of Iowa and South Dakota
of the lakes and hunting
of the children
of himself
and of the wilderness.

Swede, when you go in Summer
Back to lakes
and to the cool salvation of the trees
of Lake Bimidji
carry the soul and sound and laughter
of these song-
soul-
filled
children.

iv.
He is a man
who makes discoveries
in children
each hour of his life

who reads each word they have written
as a code word of their souls.

He is a man
who, through the cold eye of the camera,
records the love, the life-work, respect,
the deep affection
of his own heart.

Recorder of faces
Engraver of souls          O, Father . . .

Out of you
the dark night            My Father . . .
and the bright sun
of love for them          Father?

and love's life

and love's children . . .

                          My Father . . .

EYES

All of the grade schools are closed
or closing.  Windows that once exploded
with the fiery leaves of Fall,
the paper pumpkin cutouts of Halloween;
the snowmen and Santa Clauses
of another time, now stare like sow's eyes
at the changing seasons, uncomprehending
and uncaring at the foothills
the natives call mountains.

When the new school year begins, the children
pass the old school, wrapped like fat
sausages in their Fall and Winter clothes,
armed against the early cold and waiting.
The orange and black buses
pick them up on remote roads in the country
and rattle them off to a new school, 20 miles away.

The new school has bright new toilets
and electric paint along its corridors
and classrooms.  It has laboratories
with shining beakers and a learning center
filled with microfiche, film clips,
audio casettes and video.  It also has books
but these are carefully secured behind partitions
and are little used.  There are three closed circuit
television sets in the center.  They stare back,
blindly, at the students who pass by,
occasionally flickering to life—
grey, solemn, ghosts of learning past,
of "how to" and "you can" and "learning is fun."

The children go home.  Their parents ask
"What did you do in school today?"
And they say: "We watched TV and did our exercises."
Their parents look at each other
with questions in their eyes.

"They had the Fonz, talking about Shakespeare,"
the oldest one says.
The children finish their supper and are excused.
The father and mother finish their meal.
The wife brings coffee from the kitchen.
They sit, listening to
"Monday, Tuesday, Happy Days"
from the bedroom upstairs.

In the dining room, still at table,
the father stares at the complete set
of the encyclopaedia he bought
for the children.  Its volumes have remained
undisturbed since the first week after he put them in their case,
when he demonstrated how to use them.

The wife pours more coffee.
"It says in the paper they're going to reopen
the Washington School and use it again."
"Yeah," he says.  "What for?"
"I guess they're going to put in a center
of some kind for rehabilitating kids
who dropped out of school."

Chester, Massachusetts
Summer 1981

# PART SIX

# DOING THE TRAVELER'S LAUNDRY

*for Charles Levendosky and Allen Ginsburg*

Ask if he needs to have laundry done.
Chances are he will say, yes.  Three
shirts, some shorts, a tee shirt, a pair
of jeans.  He will hand you the laundry
wrapped in the chambray shirt that echoes
the Depression, farm labor, migrant workers.
You accept it as a gift, knowing that, after
the spin-dry cycle, the gas dryer, the folded
laundry; after he is gone, after his voice
no longer echoes in the basement room
among the covered pipes, the abandoned
baby crib, after all this, there remains
in your washer/dryer the oil of his body,
the soil from his hands, the dreams
of his gentleness.

# INSTRUCTIONS FOR THE TRAVELER

Don't tell them where you're going;
they will find out soon enough.
Give them news, but only the news
they would not hear from someone else.
Do not bore them with detail;
they have too much already.
Ask after their families;
but do not get to know their children.
Loving other people's sons and daughters
will drink your strength, make you old
before the spade is ready.  Do not
tell them where you've been;
they will read the news in your eyes.
And when they bend to your lips
and touch your eyes
and sing,
do not listen.

## THE TRAVELER LEARNS MANY LANGUAGES

he understands that words change things.
He grows accustomed to the tongues
of fools, academics, philosophers, hookers and hustlers,
failing, at times, to tell them apart.
He listens to lonely men in bars
talking about their daughters and sons,
the piece of ass they had in Houston
the night before, asking the barman
where the action is.  If they ask
he tells them he is on the road a lot.
Often, late at night, the words
run together, becoming one word.

## THE TRAVELER GOES HOME

The country you lived in as a child
does not look the same
when you are a traveler,
returning to it after many years.
Too much speed has blurred
the rural roads,
the main street of the town,
the lane leading into the graveyard
just outside the town, the town
where you grew old
but did not die.

Some of the faces remain.
You order a cup of coffee
at the all-night cafe
where your grandmother worked
and the waitress says:
"You used to live around here, didn't you?"
And when you nod, she says:
"Not much around here
anymore.  Everything closing down."
She mops the counter with a wet, grey towel,
smiles and goes back to the table
by the jukebox in the corner.

Outside, on the street again,
the single streetlight blurs,
the street fades into history
and you consign the future
to the rented Ford
you're driving "on travel."

A tractor-trailer rig blasts
four times on the new Interstate
that bypasses the town
where you were born
and grew old
and did not die.

# THIS IS A STRANGE CITY

the traveler says as he slides onto the barstool
in the brand new, just-opened
Ramada Inn.
                    The water gives the Cutty Sark
a chlorine taste.  A fat man
across the bar sucks
on a long cigar, curling his lips
about it as he inhales.  The barman
talks about football
and Fran Tarkenton
and his 1974 Olds Cutlass.
The waitresses are dressed in short red
pants; they have flowers in their hair.
Muzak masturbates the air, too soft
to identify, too loud to talk above.

Three men are sitting at a table
near the door.  They are talking
loudly about the Vikings and one of them
mentions Vince Lombardi.
                    Somewhere in this strange
city, the traveler says, men and women
and men and men
and women and women
are loving each other

and there is a knowledge
that will save us from cheap cigars
and Fran Tarkenton
and the Vikings
yes, even save us
from the memory of Vince Lombardi.

# THE TRAVELER IS NOT GOOD AT LONG-RANGE PLANNING

He has too many places to go, people
to see, voices to listen to
on the telephone.  His life
is a series of broken connections
and busy signals.  When in
depression, he prays,
he gets a tape recording that says:
"Sorry.  All circuits are busy."

He carries, in his mind, the mountains
of Wyoming; the small, pale flowers
of New Mexico; the grey, ghostly womb
of the Strait of Juan de Fuca.

He makes no comment
when asked what he wants from life
and writes
"Not Applicable"
when he is told to say
where he is going.

The Night is Yesterday,
the Day, Tomorrow,
Tomorrow is the Year Before.

His mind is the bookkeeper
of lost flights, missed trains,
tight connections;
there is a trail of his luggage
from LaGuardia to O'Hare.

And at Dallas/Fort Worth
he discovers he is color blind.

# PART SEVEN

CREATION
*for Doug Anderson, 1971*

The work of giants
Comes slow
Moving through catacombs and caves
Fighting waves of joy and sorrow
Falling down the eaves of half-forgotten pregnancy and birth.

When cummings' father moved
Through dooms of love
His son
Reborn
And dying followed him into the grave
Just long enough to read the rough braille of his life
And see the seasons follow it to dry dust and dead flowers.

We were as one, once, my father
And his father and the dead at Wounded Knee

Great winds blew from my father's grave
And carried me beyond the plains
Into the plainsong of conformity

Myself, My Self,
Caught in a prison made of hate
For strangers
Lied to the Me my father made
Being a stranger
Like my self

He was a big man (in photographs
worn gray by absent mother's hands,
shuttled about from trunk to cabinet to trunk)
sonofabitch he was big

And it took ten men to cart him to his grave
(but they were drunk and did not notice
there were too many of them there
the day he kissed off his mother and the black earth of
Iowa and the universe)

How many times, walking a street in a strange town
Waiting for the bars to close
And sanity's dark angel to return
Have I thought of that big man
And seen the dark hole of his final testament
And heard the voice of giants
Crashing in my mind?

Giants move slowly
As all strangers move
Working their way toward
Gentleness
And immortality.

Growing with children
Growing with love
Gnawing at the heart's black cable
Going with great steps into black, broken mountains

Waiting for the time of giants

Waiting for knowledge

Winding down the universe to fit the rhythm of their minds.

THE WIFE

This delicate barbarian beside me
Curses me, intelligently trespassing
On those simple vows I made within.
Somnambulists who cry of childhood
Desecrate the mold and press eternal
Witnesses to take the stand.  We
Cross the bed of flowers through nocturnal
Images of swallowed fire and splitting wood,
A windless symphony of lonely sin.
On, to the bed the lovely wake surpassing
Each death; beyond the pleasures of soliloquy.

## THE WORSHIP

The sadness of my life is this:
That I shall never touch you
But there will be that sudden
Defence in your eyes,
Causing your brain to see
And see me not.
The sadness in my heart is this:
That I shall not hold you
Even for the briefest moment
Lest your body twist
And tear me from myself
To fall upon you.
The sadness in my mind is this:
That I shall never kneel before you
But find your feet have turned
And fled me down these callow halls—
Christ crucified by carelessness;
The idol smashed by fear;
Hands folded in the empty space
Holding aloft your former face.

# A MATTER OF FLESH AND TIME

Ageless, you say.  And I am old at twenty-five.
Grown old beyond my face, hardly alive
And growing far more feeble with each solemn click
Of those fatal clocks we wind each night.  There is no
        trick
Of magic now to take away the awful silence of the long
Protruding lung; no simple exercise or song
To cut away the blinding tissues round the heart.
Those years that seemed so twisted and so short
Were longer years than we had thought.  The
        sleepless nights
Cost more in physical disdain than all the mortal flights
In strewn back alleys where the furious plunging alcohol
Of arguments spewed all about us, left us lying in small
Watered streams beside the walls.  It is the words,
        the drain
Of blood in rushing valvular disturbance to the brain
Amid some heated argument with you.  The kill—
Once sensed—enrages the small conscience of the will
Until at last the hunter pulls the slacking rein
Inward and needles the hounds to stop.  That pain
Which was the least has now become the final strain
Upon the heart.  Hear how the hounds bay in the final rain.

## MONA LISA

Clear, dogmatic, the mystery
of her smile turned men's heads
through ages of argument

an indecisive air about the yellowing eyes
the softly folded fingertips

a prayerful duchess or count's
mistress; finally, bad teeth

a breath of hungry seething
filled the canvas (someone said)

whose needs she filled and what
cold destiny was hers
no one could say save Leonardo

whose pen-solemn brush
had set her down for argument
and he was dead

viewed from a distance
as, of course, he did himself
objectively
the eyes are all-seeing
yet seem not to see
or to have seen

the floods of Florence
have come and gone
in Venice the water is rising
inch by inch against the worn stone
of our history

smile, as you did then, shall do forever
art is yesterday
licking at tomorrow's breast
muttering among the muddy waters

love?   passion?   later.   later.

THE LEPERS
*for E. L. Mayo*

The lepers rise with us
in morning
their great ochre and saffron
eyes gaze at us.  They are merci-
less.  Their voices rise like howling
birds.  They form a mass
together.  They demand we wash
their open wounds
with vinegar and aloes.
They cry for brine when we give them
water.  We are in
the city.  They follow us
past citadels of culture
past abandoned subway stations.
Through official tunnels
to the ends of avenues.
The monuments and memorials
of the city are unclean.
They cannot be cleaned.
We are told they would crumble.
The lepers sit in the shadow
of statues of men on horses.
The position of the horses' hooves
tell us how their masters
died/in bed/in triumph/in service
of their/country/in times of peace
and times of non/peace.

The lepers are insatiable
they seek our feet
they petition us with ashes
we breathe in deeply
and do not breathe again.

And do not breathe

again.

# TRANSFORMATIONS
*for Richard Howard*

And something in your language
dances on the edge of music
keeping time with Gide and Sappho
aching for the silences of Hindemith or Mahler

where do you go when the words fail, fall
in the cubicles where words do not exist?

where do you lie when language does not
come, like music, like the fall of suns?

when the stars fail and the edge of night
betrays you in sunlight?  When the words
flow and will not stop?  When the language
overtakes you, kills your tongue,
betrays the last light of the other
language?


●


When, in the light, the lap of language
where the sounds inch toward older meaning
do you pass, and if you do, pause enough
to hear the last word
see the lost line
in its last coffin
of
     language?


●

140

Enough of that.  Letters sent
to other people.  Letters left
unopened on tables by doorways
in a hundred mansions.  Say
what is left to say.  Make it
gleam like amethyst in dying suns.
Converse.  Take pen in hand.
Send letters.  Do not wait
for answers.

## MAKER OF STONE

*for Ron Dunham*

i.
You are the home
of the form, the molder,
the maker of stone
in whose hands
stone becomes the shape
of life, of art and love
and dignity.

ii.
I have seen stone
flat on a mountain,
hanging from precipices,
grey-grained, blotched with red
and black, whiter than cumulus,
thunderous, bold
and gaunt in shards
of blackness.

iii.
Yet I had not seen
stone
until I watched
the chisel in your hand,
saw the fiery splinters
peel and drop away.
Then, in one sharp,
final blow, saw how the metal
pierced the grey-white grain
and opened up

the universe

of stone.

## ON LIVING/ON DYING/ON BEING OF USE

*for Bruce Walters*

i.
When you were a child
I remember how detached
you sometimes were, when,
in a room with other people
your eyes seemed focused
far beyond them, almost in another
time, your ears testing the sounds
of voices long removed.

I thought, then, that your silences
were silences of beauty
and of majesty.

ii.
When you went to Nam
I thought of you, often,
and your silences.
In the center of that horror
how your eyes must strain
not to see.  How your ears must have drowned
themselves in some remembered
sound to blot out Death's staccato.

I thought, then, that your silences
were your salvation,
your giver of life.

iii.
When you came home
I did not see you.  I heard,
from your mother and your

father, that you seemed changed,
that you were a different Bruce
than we had known.  They mentioned
an occasional silence.  And the serious
way you sometimes stared at others.

I thought, then, that your silences
would carry you back,
would keep you going.


iv.
When, trapped in fire,
being of use to others, your flesh
burned as you had seen the children
burn, when the screams you had blocked
from your mind came to you and not even the metal
of the needle could take them away,
when silence seemed not enough
to save you, the will announced itself
the savior, the final testament.


v.
You say: What does it matter?
I say: You must make it matter.
You say: What if I do not care?
I say: Others care.  You say:
It is not enough.  I say: It is enough
if you make it enough.  You say:
It is my life.  I say: And the life
of others.  You say: I do not want anyone
else to die as I have seen helpless people
die.  I do not want someone I love
to suffer.  I say: Losing you would be more
suffering than we who love you could endure.
You say: I can refute all of your arguments.

I say: Live, and refute them.

I am not infallible.

vi.
When you were a child
I remember how detached
you were.  Now I see that you are not
different, that the flood that raged
inside you, then, still rages.
That the good and gentle and beautiful
child you were, grows still in this man
you are.  That you are, as you were,
a being in whom light shines,
from whom light comes,
through whom I have come to understand

silence.

# AN OPEN LETTER TO THE POETS OF AMERICA

I believe in you more than you believe in you.
I believe in you because it is necessary
for someone to believe in you more than
you believe in your selves.

I believe in you because you have taken poetry
     by the throat
and turned it around in the dark corners and alleys
of our lives and made it Sun again.

I believe in you because, without you,
the young men/women of the sixties
would not have had a voice
to stop the blood or cancel kings
who called themselves Presidents.

I believe in you because you are
Tom McGrath and Denise Levertov
and Maxine Kumin and William Meredith

and because you are Michael Moos and Ramona Weeks
and Jenne Andrews and Ken McCullough.

I believe in you because you take the
work of God and make it your work.

I believe in you because you are fire
and words made fire.  And felons.  And victims.

I believe in you because it is necessary
that someone believe in that part of you
that says what America must say
but does not say

or will not say
without you.  I believe in you
more than you believe in you
because you are necessary
and nothing will replace you.

Not even memory.

PIECES
*for Judy Hogan*


THE DOORKNOB

Perfectly round
without blemish
burnished to a soft glow
in the ghostly lights of night
turned once
releases the invisible
chalice of morning.


THE TABLE

Great oval, two-leafed
native of a square room,
whispers as I write.
Bereft of plates,
of steaming food,
of cups and saucers,
stainless flatware,
paper napkins,
becoming acquainted
by accident with
words.


THE CHAIR

This chair has become a mirror of its owner's
anatomy.  It groans,
growing accustomed
to this alien form
of mine.

## THE CARPET

Inheritor of soles
of feet, of boots,
of sandals, sand worked
into its dimly oriental
patterns, covers the grain of the life
of this
house.

## THE WALLPAPER

Some mad acrylic artist
has spent some time here.
He has left brush strokes
on the bedroom, like barter,
like braille.

## THE PHOTOGRAPH

This is the father's
father, dead of emphysema
these fifteen years.
From his early manhood
he looks down upon the children
of his son, seems to be saying:
I could not carry you longer.
Now you understand.

THE STAIRCASE

It is an old house.
It has voices.  Some
of them come down the stairs
in the early morning,
whispering of ancient breakfasts,
men in morning coats,
girls with angelic faces
lisp their way through
the living room,
speaking of the boat ride
to Victoria.


THE PALM

It is 44 degrees.
Outside the window
a lone palm tree
glistens in early dew.
A nagging horn warns
of fog, of danger, of disaster.
There will be rain today
and the fog will survive it.
And the palm, like some tourist
from Abilene
will endure.


THE HOUSE

Nothing about our lives
convinces us more that
other people are our lives
than living in other people's
houses.

# POEM FOR MOLLY'S SON

It is late.
Your mother has
gone to bed
and left me in this room
that is undeniably yours.
And, being a stranger
I do not even know your name
only that you are one of two sons
no longer here
in this cool angular house
whose corridors are filled with warm washing
music of the wind through open windows.
Away at university
learning the braille of your own soul,
learning, perhaps, that no one else will touch it
or learn it with you.

Do not know you, yes.
Yet feel I do
for I am surrounded by you
and your heart and head.

One poster on the wall quotes
lyndon baines johnson
against a photograph of white helmeted police
and bloodied heads

    "Our foreign policy must
      always be an extension of
      this nation's domestic policy.
      Our safest guide to what we
      do abroad is a good
      look at what we are doing
      at home."

Remembering Chicago, your Chicago
May Day
the oldness in me
remembers too the shotguns
aimed at Walter Reuther
Sacco, Vanzetti, Eugene Debs
the herds of Nisei huddled in trucks
waiting to be taken to detention
somewhere beyond the coast
where they cannot send signals or give comfort
to aliens in a tongue they do not know

Remembering, the room becomes
a tomb of our abandoned rhetoric

There are other posters on the walls
as there are always in young rooms
Posters of the dead, the damned, the dying

Jimi, deathlike, staring from the mask of his perpetual salvation
Miles, ready for all comers, in the ring
dying in remembered sounds of greatness
and no one listening.  And Malcolm, one last raised fist,
one defiant finger to the mob
saying

       Hear me.  Hear me.
       Listen.

It is your room
and I come to it as a stranger
as a man whose countries of compassion
you would not want
or understand
knowing, as you must know,

that we are what we hate
preparing myself for this bed
hesitantly, like someone over forty
asked to undertake swimming
for the first time

Here, in the small world of your ideas,
your frustrations, your dreams
I fold my conscience carefully inside myself
warm within your hopes, your bitterness, your dreams
and fall to dreamless sleep.

Bidding good night to those who died
and those who live
weeping for kings who run mad
at play's end shrieking
*Give me some light!*

Good night.

# READING A POEM BY KEN McCULLOUGH

The skin is there.  And the muscle.
Bones break
and shove their way
through skin
and muscle.
Some of the blood
crawls between the lines.
The ink is black blood.  The paper,
muscle.  And you are
blood
and bone.
And break.

Even in these words
flat on paper

you breathe.

DEAD LETTER OFFICE

When she was twenty, she wrote
a letter to the world and, getting
no response, continued writing.
All those letters, numberless
and tight, etched in the paper
in her forthright Palmer method
pen, returned to her and, feeding
on the words that no one else would read,
she made a dialogue of monologue
of epilog of prologue
a storm of white pages whirled
about her body—when she touched them
they melted, turned to stone.
Around her face, around her body
fingers probed to find her postage.
She did not respond.  Sitting
in the twilight room of her father's house
she smiled and waited for the postman.
He whistled gently on his way past
her father's house.  He did not stop.
He also waited.  The white storm
flew about his body, a fusillade of shells
a cacophony of maggots.  And when he touched
them, they melted, and turned to stone.

## BULLETS
*for Muriel Rukeyser*

We must not let our poets
see our atrocities.  They
take the blood, distill it
into ink and spew it back
at us like bullets.  Their
words are everywhere.  There
are no eradicators strong
enough to dull them once they
strike the paper, split
our brains.
                The poet
finds the fingerprints
connects the evidence
breaks the story
prematurely.  He wrecks
the chance for prosecution.
He does not care.
He is the muckraker
of his century.  He hears
the lies and turns them into
adders, lizards, scorpions
of words.  He walks
the streets, setting his feet
down carefully between the
rot, the garbage, the blood,
the maggots we have deposited.
He is not cleansed
by water or by fire.
He uses pus for ink.
He purifies himself
condemning foul air
and thievery.  He sings

off-key to tell us
there is no harmony.
He kills each word
and knows that death's
last phone bill will
be unpaid.  He disconnects
from society.  Becomes alien
wood in the flood, floating,
dodging, bobbing downstream.
He sees us as we are.
He tells us what we are.
Even the blind
                 poet
smells and feels and hears
the ubiquitous cesspit
we've become.  O, do not
let him see.

THINGS I WANT TO SAY TO YOU

Things I want to say to you this morning
Are just the same things I have said
        at other times
Same syllables
Same sounds
The same inflections you have heard
A hundred times before.

And yet
the morning's not the same
the edging light across the window sill
of yet another motel
is not like we have seen —
cold, cutting and impersonal
it does not seem to be Light

only an intruder in the dark brush
of conversation with you.

A day comes on me
leaping, unwanted, sprawling
as a weary, tear-stained child
willful, waiting for fulfillment.

A new day,
animal, filled with pain,
flamed by wanting,
stilled by wet memory

and we become the day together
miles apart and centuries beyond
the first whisper in my waking mind

wanting to say

the same sounds
the same syllables

in the cold, hard, rain-raked
morning
of my middle years.

## LOST IN THE MAIL
*for K. M.*

Dear former jock:

O.K.  So now you play softball
and now you win trophies for fielding

I know you well enough
you never miss the high ball
or the line drive

you never get the sun in your eyes

you reach and run backward
better than I can run
forward

your lungs are heavy with air
and your feet do not turn in
upon each other

your back is like oak

some inner wind makes your muscles pitch
like waves.  you are always in motion
even when you stand, waiting, for the batter
to swing.  even when he bunts

you are alive like lava
leaping toward imagined runs
high pop flies

you catch the ball.  it is like fire.
you twist in midair.  your hand whips

down, a flame on the blue sky.
even at 1,000th of a second
the camera will not stop you
on the film.
                    you descend
an arcing angel                         !you write a poem.
a flaring hawk                            it does not stammer
in air, upon the grass                   in the sun.
and fly                                   its eye sees into
          like Pegasus                  those who

into the heart of the heart             read it!
of the sun

you cannot stop.  you cannot enter
that other kingdom where men
imagine themselves to be im-
mortal.  you are mortal.  you rake
the sweat from your forehead
casting it down
upon the splintered grass.

you blink.  you quickly smile.
you look toward second base.
you wait for the batter                 /you read a poem.
to swing
or bunt.

you crouch briefly                      /your voice is soft
close your eyes
against the sun.                          and muscle.

you meditate instantly                  /you are more than
come back from meditation
                                          light.

your eyes are a map
of the sky of Montana

your body is a universe
the earth has not discovered.


you are the most complete

and complex

poem

you will ever write.

are more than

sun.


/you are

running backward

glaring at

the sun.

you

/catch.

SPEECH
*for Robert, a stutterer who failed the third grade twice*

We are all inarticulate.
In the morning.  In the night.
The words won't come.
We try.  But something in us stops
the breath.  The tongue.  The form.
And substance of words
we want to give to others—those we love,
those who anger us, those who reach
out
eager to be part of us, at one with us,
at peace.
With words that speak love
or remembrance.

A simple statement coils upon itself
in our lungs,
upon our tongues
until, at last, we speak it, and are free.

So much of life is silence.
We learn to live with it like stones
upon the chest
ashes in the lungs.

There is, in silence, the language
few men learn to speak
and do not hear.

This, then, is a gift for you.
The silent prayer that holds your silence
as warmth and gentleness.
The world of written language

to be read in silence
when you are in pain.
The smile that does not die.
The hand that will not waver.

Peace, friend, and words to hold

or give

to others.

SON

The son I never had
is in Toronto;
he cannot come home.
He is imprisoned by an act
of conscience he was not cowardly
enough to deny.
He may live his life out
in Toronto, with his conscience,
while our guilt keeps us homeless
in his land.

The son I never had
now has a hundred dollar habit;
once a day he trails fire
through his veins, forgetting pain,
denying fear.  He has no home,
no hate, no father;
holds no truth
but one lie in his blood.

He falls through flame
and being, like a shot bird
to the water.

The son I never had
writes letters from Attica
with holes where words have been;
from Florence, Arizona and Jessup, Maryland.
He has not seen the sky for days;
the prison smells of death and rotting silences.

In Waupun, he stamps the metal plates
for rich men's cars, for yours and mine,

and waits to get approval for a transfer
to a camp near woods and good air
where he may once more call him self
creator and man.

The son I never had
is in a schoolhouse
in North Dakota.
He brings poems from the hands
of small children in dim classrooms.
Their eyes impale him.
Their hands touch him, tearing at his skin.
He is reading his own poems,
showing a carved bird in full-wing,
to the children of Havre,
and Port Townsend and Lovelock.
They set their lives down in lines.
He reads them aloud, saying:
"That is beautiful."
They are the splendor.  He is the poem.
He is like Whitman with the wounded.
Through him they write letters to themselves.

# BOOKS BY THEIR COVERS

You did not come from a large family.
Therefore, it is something new to you.
After a while you forget that they
are hand-me-down clothes,
second-hand embodiments of someone else's past.
They become a part of you,
like the second skin that comes
after heavy sunburn.
Eventually, even the odor of the former owner
disappears, strangled by floods of Bold 3 or Tide
and Clorox 2.  And when they are worn in the presence
of your friends, you no longer wonder which of them *really*
knows that the shirt you are wearing came from the Temple
Israel Thrift Shop on Wisconsin Avenue.  It is *your* shirt;
it has the color, the stripe, the configurations
of style and comfort you recognized
when you picked it out of the pile of discards
in the dim second floor of the shop on Wisconsin Avenue,
only a short bus ride from Lord and Taylor and the riding-breech
ladies of Georgetown.  It grows older, with you;
and when, like you, it has come to threads around the neck
you keep it only to wear around the house,
comfortable as an old friend, one who knows your neck cricks,
your back spasms; one who can be trusted to smile
at you warmly from the mirror as you reluctantly shave.
And, when it is truly beyond wearing, you put it in the back
of the bottom bureau drawer, refusing to use it for dusting
or mopping up spills when the paper towels are gone.
Like a cow who is too old to milk, too feeble to calve,
you put it to pasture.  Like what is left of your life,
you hang onto it; you will not throw it away.

## WIND OVER ASHES
*for Pier Paolo Pasolini*


In the shadow of the eye's grim delight,
Desire's angelic muscles:
Men, women, children, murmuring

> *Take me*
>> *Take me . . .*

Wakening, fire-filled and bursting
From the awkward harness of society
In one faultless eruption
Where volcanic ash lays waste to countries.

Come to tell us we are flawed,
Imperfect resurrections of some god-like whim
Living in a cave of hope, less necessary
Than the lava of theology, the peasant's diadem.

Memory, like wind over ashes
The particles of flesh,
Smoke of the mind, stirring,
Sifted, sorted in
the winding sheet of the wind.

Angel's fire becalmed as water
In shifting wind becomes the sidelong
Glance of sexual compassion.
We are alone with flame and learning.

Burning silently in fields
Nettle clutching at our flesh
We put down the flame
Becoming painter, whore, mystic,

Pederast, catatonic ministers, sisters of the poor,
Recording in an endless work:
God's children muttering

   *Take me*

       *Take me* . . .

Photograph by Jan T. Randolph

LEONARD RANDOLPH was born August 1, 1926, in Leon, Iowa. He lived his early years with his mother's parents on a dirt farm in Northern Missouri; attended elementary grades one through four in a one-room schoolhouse near Saline, MO; grades five through nine in schools in Leon, IA, and high school in Lorimor, IA. In Lorimor, he founded the school's first student newspaper and worked full-time for *The Lorimor Journal,* the only weekly newspaper in the area, where he operated a Linotype, wrote ads for local merchants, covered the 'news' and wrote a novella called "Storm over Hollywood," which was serialized in the *Journal.* "On his own" from age 14, he left high school at the end of his junior year, having attained enough 'credits' for graduation the following year. Waiting to enter the armed services, he worked for a year as a spray painter in a defense factory, wrote ads and press releases for three movie theatres and worked the graveyard shift as a short order cook in a downtown cafe in Marshalltown, Iowa, simultaneously.

He served as a combat infantryman in the 7th Division in the Pacific during World War II. At the end of the war, he was transferred to the Public Information Section of the United States Army Military Government in Korea, the occupation army. While serving there, he wrote and was assistant producer of the first radio drama-serial broadcast over the Seoul Broadcasting System—a series based loosely on the patterns of Jack Armstrong and Little Orphan Annie established by radio in the U.S. and designed to provide information to the general Korean audience.

Following his discharge from the service, he worked for a time as a clerk in a men's clothing store and then enrolled full-time under the GI Bill at Drake University in Des Moines, Iowa, where he majored in English with a minor in radio journalism. The latter course led to an immediate audition with a commercial radio station in Des Moines where he was employed full-time as announcer, news writer-commentator, disc jockey and producer/narrator of a series of programs broadcasting poetry and readings from Shakespeare and the *Bible.*

He moved to the East in 1951 and went to work as a general news reporter and press photographer for a daily newspaper in Stroudsburg, Pennsylvania, eventually concentrating heavily on education news reporting, human interest features, film, drama and book reviewing. His work on the county education system brought awards to the newspaper from the Pennsylvania Newspaper Publishers Association and led to the job of publications editor for the Pennsylvania State Library. This, in turn, brought him to the job of Special Assistant to the Lieutenant Governor and, a year later, to his work as Press Secretary and speechwriter for Governor David L. Lawrence during his four year term.

He then became Executive Director of the Shapp Education Foundation for one year and took leave of absence from that job to manage the successful Congressional campaign (Democratic) in his home (PA) district. He was offered the position of administrative assistant to the newly-elected Congressman; moved to Washington and worked on Capitol Hill for three years, during which time he became interested in and assisted with the campaign to create a National Foundation on the Arts and the Humanities on the House side.

Shortly after the National Endowment for the Arts was created in September, 1965, he went to work for the new agency as an assistant to Chairman Roger L. Stevens, dealing primarily with Congressional liaison. Thereafter, in rapid order, he became Assistant Director of State and Community Programs and, in 1970 was named Director of Literature Programs for the National Endowment by Chairman Nancy Hanks. He retained this position until 1979, when he left the Endowment and the Federal Government, spending most of his remaining time in work on a novel and the collection of this volume of poems. During his employment with the National Endowment he voluntarily refused to submit work of any kind for publication since he was associated, on a professional, grants-making basis with the small, independent presses with whom he would have chosen to be associated as a writer.

First published, as a poet, in *Symbol*, the Drake University student creative writing magazine, he then had work accepted by and published in *Accent*, *The University of Kansas City Review* (now *New Letters*), *Epos*, the *New York Herald Tribune* and other small, literary magazines during the 1950's.

His interest in theatre, as an avocation and a possible profession, took firm roots in Des Moines with appearances in *The Heiress* and other plays in Kendall Community Playhouse. It was an interest carried further in community theatres and professional summer stock in the East where he has been seen as the lead in *Abe Lincoln In Illinois*, Stanley Kowalski in *A Streetcar Named Desire*, Christopher Wren in Agatha Christie's *The Mousetrap*, Jeff in *Brigadoon*, Mr. Applegate in *Damn Yankees*, Tom in *The Glass Menagerie*, Johnny and Polo in *A Hatful of Rain*, Malvolio in *Twelfth Night*, *Richard II*, King Henry IV and as The Emperor in the American premiere of William Golding's *The Brass Butterfly*. He has also directed and produced numerous workshop productions and staged readings of new and little-known plays in community theatres.

During his term of employment with the National Endowment for the Arts he was responsible for the creation and nurturing of a nationwide program placing (generally younger) professional poets and fiction writers in elementary and secondary classrooms throughout the nation. He considers this work the major achievement of his days with the Federal agency since it brought him into constant contact with writers and the state arts agencies who provided them with employment.

He has been married and is the father of two daughters, Jan and Ann. He is also a grandfather. He and his wife, the former Gloria Shafer, were divorced in 1974.

Designed and typeset at Bull City Studios, Durham, North Carolina.
Printed in an edition of 1000 copies at Braun-Brumfield,
  Ann Arbor, Michigan.